LONDON COUNTRY BUSES
IN COLOUR

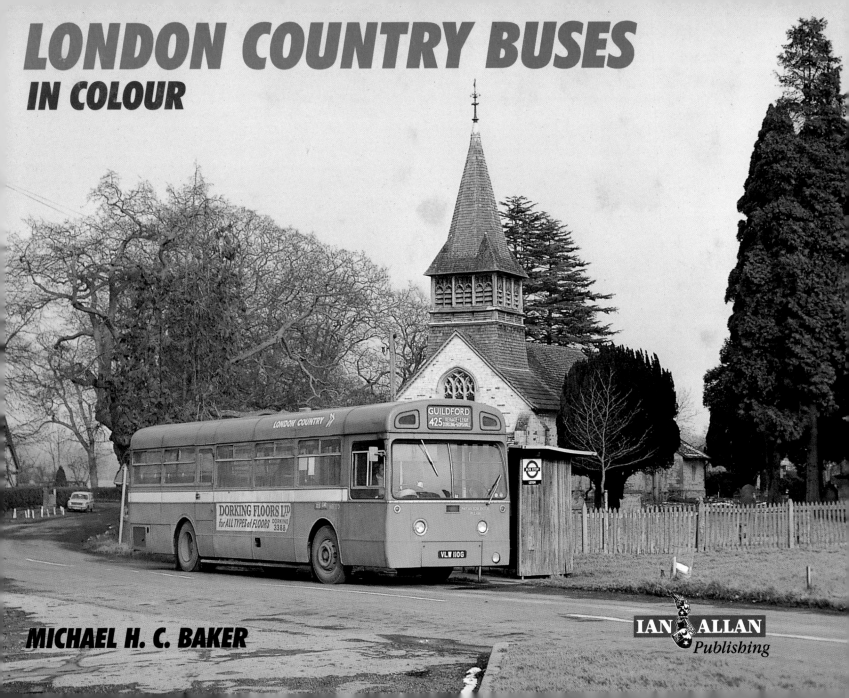

MICHAEL H. C. BAKER

IAN ALLAN Publishing

Introduction

For those who did not know the London Country bus and the area it served particularly well, it was not necessarily the animal its title suggested. Certainly, London's green buses could be seen deep in the rural areas and the pleasant market towns of the Home Counties, but they were much more commonly found in the capital's outer suburbs. Take, for instance, the route I most often travelled upon, the 403. It set off from Wallington, past Payne's chocolate factory, round the back of Croydon Gas Works, through the heart of Croydon, a county borough of some quarter of a million inhabitants and then up the northern face of the North Downs, which was mostly covered in desirable residences built between the two world wars. It was only when it got to Chelsham Garage, home for many of the buses which worked the route, that it finally entered countryside proper. It was later cut back to Chelsham and for a time in the 1980s passed, quite logically, to a red bus company.

The truly rural routes seldom made money and were subsidised by the suburban ones, which is one reason why so many of them no longer see buses or are worked by concerns structured very differently from London Transport, once the largest operator of public transport in the world.

Although London Transport came into existence on 1 July 1933, it wasn't until early the following year that all the independents in the Country Area passed into its control. In October that year a new route numbering system came into existence: 300-399 for all the green routes north of the Thames, 400-499 for those south of the river. Remnants of this system can still be detected.

Throughout the 1930s large numbers of Chiswick-designed buses and coaches replaced the motley collection the LPTB had inherited. Postwar RT production got under way in 1947, 1948 as far as the Country Area was concerned, and the many RTs featured in these pages are testimony to the quality and longevity of this classic design.

Although the Central and Country Areas shared many common designs, there were some that were exclusive to one or the other, most noticeably the Green Line and private hire fleets. Whilst the double-decker always predominated, the Country Area made considerable use of single-deckers, including the last forward-control buses ordered by London Transport, the little 26-seat GSs of 1953. But just as the RT was the backbone of the double-deck fleet, so the RF outnumbered by a considerable margin all other single-deckers. It has to be said that the livery of Lincoln green and a single pale cream band was not particularly imaginative, and as soon as London Country came into existence in 1970 things began to get a little brighter.

London Country has often been likened to a Polo mint, its territory being roughly circular with a big hole in the middle which was central London, although its Green Line fleet did cut right through this. The 1970s were not happy times for the bus industry. AEC, the traditional supplier of London's buses, merged with leyland; its final bus design, the single-deck Merlin of which London Country had a couple of hundred, being a disaster. The unreliability of Leyland's products was sowing the seeds of its own demise; car ownership was booming, particularly in the affluent outer-London suburbs and the Home Counties; and in order to cut costs London Country went over to one-person-operation as quickly as possible. The RT's successor, the Routemaster, was nothing like as long-lived in its London Country versions, the Green Line vehicles being demoted to buses and the whole fleet being disposed of by 1980, most of it back to London Transport. The era of the specially designed London bus was over and from then on a London Country vehicle would look no different from those found in many other parts of the UK, although, of course, the livery would distinguish it.

The first break with tradition in this respect came with the repainting of

Front cover: Lincoln green-liveried Daimler XF4 in Bell Street, Reigate in October 1965. *Roy Hobbs*

Back cover: SM464 of Dartford Garage at Dartford on 19 August 1978. Introduced in the Country Area in 1970, the AEC Swifts reached a total of 838 in London Transport and London Country service. To be strictly accurate, their immediate predecessors — the MBs, the MBSs and the MBAs — were also known as Swifts by their manufacturers, but London called them Merlins. The 36ft-long Merlins proved to be too long for many routes, hence the shortened, 33ft 5in-long Swift. Both types proved to be little short of disastrous. They were mechanically unreliable, their bodies leaked, the heating system was temperamental and even the paint refused to stay in place. It was a sad end to the long association of AEC with London's red and green buses. Less than a year after this picture was taken, SM464 went the way of so many of its brethren, to Wombwell Diesels scrapyard near Barnsley. *Geoff Rixon*

Title page: MB110 outside Leigh parish church on a bracing February afternoon in 1976. *Roy Hobbs*

First published 1998

ISBN 0 7110 2557 6

Published by Ian Allan Publishing

an imprint of Ian Allan Ltd, Terminal House, Station Approach, Shepperton, Surrey TW17 8AS.
Printed by Ian Allan Printing Ltd at its works at Coombelands in Runnymede, England.

Code: 9802/B3

Daimler Fleetlines — in sky blue for a new commuter service in Stevenage New Town — by London Transport just before it handed over to London Country at the beginning of 1970. Gradually, as the story unfolds in these pages, Lincoln green fades away, sometimes almost literally. Deregulation brought about the break-up of London Country in 1986 and today the distinction between what used to be the red Central and the green Country Area of London Transport is far less clear. However, the preservationists have done us proud and, thanks to them, the once familiar sounds, shapes and liveries can still be seen from time to time in London's country.

Acknowledgements

Apart from my own records and recollections, I have consulted many sources: Ian Allan Publishing *ABC*s, Ken Blacker's *RT Story* and his two-part history of the Routemaster, Ken Glazier's *RF*, D. W. K. Jones and B. J. Davis's *Green Line 1930-80*, LOTS journals and much else. I am most grateful to the photographers whose work graces these pages: Dave Brown, D. T. Elliott, Roy Hobbs, Geoff Lumb, Dick Riley and Geoff Rixon. Peter Plummer, Chairman of the London Bus Preservation Trust and joint owner of the superbly preserved RT593, has been a great help, as have others at Cobham Bus Museum.

Right: Gravesend, 19 April 1976. RML2326 overtakes SMA18. No standard Routemasters were ever delivered new to the Country Area, and it wasn't until 1965 that green-painted RMLs went into service. RML2326 was delivered to Northfleet Garage in November of that year and it is seen here in original livery — apart from the bright yellow London Country stripe. It is still at work, from the Clapton Garage of Cowie Leaside Buses on Route 38.

The 21 SMAs looked quite different from any previous Green Line coaches, being AEC Swifts fitted with 36ft-long, 45-seat Alexander bodies — the first time the Scottish bodybuilder had won a London contract. In fact, they rather sneaked into London, for they had been ordered by South Wales Transport and were diverted to London Country in the spring of 1972. The 725 was a favourite haunt of the class during its fairly brief life with London Country.
R. C. Riley

Above: Seen at the same spot on the same day is BN26. Ordered as replacements for the RFs — although never as numerous — the BNs were 7ft 6in-wide Bristol LHS6Ls with ECW 35-seat bodies, which first entered service in 1974, following the initial batch of similar 8ft-wide BLs of 1973. The standard Bristol/ECW product, familiar for so long in many parts of the country, had never before been a feature of the London scene other than in exceptional circumstances, although ECW had built bodies for London buses from time to time. Best known in the Country Area had been the little 26-seat, forward-control Guy GSs of 1953. *R. C. Riley*

Right: RT593 gleams in the midsummer sun beneath Box Hill. Although RTs were long-familiar at this Surrey beauty spot, the 480 was a Kentish route operated by Dartford Garage. RT593 represents the first type of standard postwar double-decker, with a Weymann roof number-box body dating from 1948. It is preserved at Cobham. *M. H. C. Baker*

Left: Mainstay of the Green Line fleet until displaced by RFs was the 10T10 — 266 of these handsome vehicles being introduced in 1938. Many of the AEC Regals with Chiswick-built bodies served as ambulances or with the US forces during the war. Most returned when Green Line services restarted in 1946. Downgraded to buses on the arrival of the RFs, they ended their days with London Transport as staff buses in 1955/6. The lone survivor is T504, another Cobham resident, seen carrying blinds for the 701 Gravesend to Ascot parked early on a summer Sunday morning amongst the greenery opposite the Tate Gallery on Millbank, a spot it would have passed every day whilst working this route.

I once asked a driver of a 10T10 what sort of speed he could reach and whether it was possible, out in the country, to exceed the PSV legal limit of 30mph. He replied that as no speedometers were fitted, he didn't know: 'I go the same speed as everyone else and hope for the best'. *M. H. C. Baker*

Right: A most unlikely looking London Country bus stands in the forecourt of Northfleet Garage on 22 June 1975. It is a Burlingham-bodied Leyland Titan PD3, originally built for Ribble in 1957. A batch was bought in 1975 by London Country for its training fleet. The former Ribble No 1515 has not yet been repainted into yellow learner livery. *R. C. Riley*

Left: The mid-1970s was a sad time for maintenance standards on London Country. The fleet it had inherited from London Transport was getting long — in some cases very long — in the tooth, and many of its new buses were proving unreliable. Vehicles had to be hired from a number of sources in a not totally successful attempt to maintain schedules. This is a rather handsome Eastbourne Corporation AEC Mark V Regent of 1956 fitted with an East Lancs body, working from Northfleet Garage on 19 April 1976. *R. C. Riley*

Right: Red and green meet at Green Street Green on 14 April 1973: London Country RF548 from Dunton Green Garage and London Transport RT956 of Sidcup Garage. *R. C. Riley*

Left: Dunton Green's RF684 heads through Sevenoaks on a sunny October morning in 1973. The poster advertising Green Line bargains hardly improves its handsome lines. The RF, the single-deck equivalent of the RT, took up work in London in 1951, and was almost as long-lived, the last not being withdrawn from service with London Country until July 1979. *R. C. Riley*

Above: A fairly unexpected type drafted in to help solve London Country's troubles was this Royal Blue coach, a Bristol MW6G of 1967, fitted with a somewhat ungainly ECW 39-seat body. It is seen here at Sevenoaks bus station, laying over between bus duties from Dunton Green Garage in February 1977. *D. T. Elliott*

Below: Another view of a former Ribble PD3. This one, seen at Sevenoaks in August of 1976, has been repainted into the bright yellow livery used by the National Bus Company's training fleet. It stands alongside a Maidstone & District Northern Counties-bodied Daimler Fleetline of 1964, which is about to set off to the Kent county town of Maidstone. *D. T. Elliott*

Right: SMA5 heads through Shortlands near Dick Riley's home on its long journey through the South London suburbs from Gravesend to Windsor on 9 February 1975. The stepped-up seats, rising towards the rear, can be seen clearly; there seems to be few people sitting in them, which is somewhat atypical as this route did excellent business, providing a reasonably fast link between towns such as Dartford, Sidcup, Bromley, Croydon, Sutton, Kingston and Staines, where few direct rail services operated. *R. C. Riley*

Left: The unrelieved NBC green does nothing for East Grinstead's RF226, standing amongst the slush on a grey January day in 1973 outside Oxted station, the terminus of the 494. Originally a Green Line coach dating from April 1952, it was downgraded to a bus in November 1965. It was withdrawn from Leatherhead Garage in July 1974. *M. H. C. Baker*

Right: East Grinstead and Godstone garages shared the operation of the 409, a route which terminated at its southern end at Forest Row on the edge of the Ashdown Forest, and at its northern end at West Croydon. Godstone also worked the 411, a route which ran from West Croydon to Reigate by way of Godstone and Redhill, jointly with Reigate Garage. Here, a couple of immaculate green RTs, 3127 of Godstone on the 409 and Reigate's 3048 on the 411, both delivered in 1950, and Catford's red RT4679, stand beside West Croydon station in April 1959. Just visible above the rear green RT is the turning loop of the 630 trolleybuses. *M. H. C. Baker*

Right: A view from the upper deck of an RT, familiar to passengers in the Home Counties for over 30 years, as it heads along a tree-lined country main road. *M. H. C. Baker*

Left: RCL2244 approaches the West Croydon terminus of the 414 at the end of its long run from Horsham on 18 February 1975. The RCLs ousted the RTs from this route early in 1972; they stayed some five years before being replaced by Leyland Nationals. *R. C. Riley*

Above: Yet another type drafted in to help keep London Country operational in the mid-1970s was this Weymann-bodied Daimler Fleetline of Bournemouth Corporation, dating from 1965. It is seen here at West Croydon on 6 January 1976. Open-top, red-painted versions of these worked the Round London Sightseeing Tour for a time. *R. C. Riley*

Right: AF4 at the Bromley terminus of the 410, 19 March 1977. Eleven of these Northern Counties-bodied Daimler Fleetlines were delivered to Godstone Garage in 1972, from which they worked until withdrawal in 1980. They had been intended for Western Welsh. A London Transport DMS stands behind AF4. *R. C. Riley*

Left: Another route which passed through Croydon, and for much of its distance ran parallel with the 470, was the 408. Leatherhead's RT2504 stands ready to depart from Chelsham Garage, surrounded by refurbished Green Line RFs, in the summer of 1971. The newly overhauled 21-year-old double-decker, adorned with the London Country symbol, bright canary yellow band and fleetname, had been delivered to Dunton Green in February 1950. The entire batch 2499-2521 served Croydon when new, and RT2504 was the last green survivor, all the others having been repainted red or withdrawn. *M. H. C. Baker*

Below: A vastly sadder scene at Chelsham, some six years later: RT4747, an unidentified RT minus engine, RT628 and RT2777 stand shabby and neglected out of service in May 1977. *M. H. C. Baker*

Left: A fascinating use for a former bus: uniform store No 581J seen at Chelsham on 29 May 1976. It began its career in 1952 as a more or less standard provincial lowbridge Weymann-bodied AEC Regent, RLH44. *R. C. Riley*

Right: Four very different types at Chelsham in the summer of 1977. Nearest the camera is RT1018, next is a Maidstone Borough Council Massey-bodied Atlantean hired to help out on the 403, a Leyland National Green Line coach and former double-deck coach RMC1511. *M. H. C. Baker*

A scene from Chelsham in June 1977. From left to right: RT604, RCL2240 and RT1018. The painting of RTs into full National livery right at the end of their careers took practically everyone by surprise. As the winter of 1977 drew to an end there was only one RT left in regular passenger service with London Country: RT3536, at Chelsham. Then, in April, RT1018 suddenly reappeared, newly overhauled in pale green. In the case of most companies the application of NBC green was a retrograde step, but many considered that when applied to RTs it was a great improvement over the hitherto somewhat sombre London Country Lincoln green.

A little later an equally splendid RT3461 took up service from Chelsham and finally the trio was completed by RT604. This was nominally the oldest of them all, belonging to the very first group of green RTs, having arrived at Hemel Hempstead in July 1948. Enthusiasts came from far and wide to see them.
M. H. C. Baker

Right: 1977 was very much an Indian summer for the trio as by early 1978 RT3461, seen here in March of that year, had been relegated to learner duties, and by June all had finished passenger service. Thus, the story of RT operation by London Country came to an end, RT604 missing its 30 years by just one month. All three have been preserved and RT604 is still sometimes seen in its NBC livery at its old haunts, for it now belongs to the Purley Transport Preservation Group. *M. H. C. Baker*

Below: Three buses which had far shorter lives are seen on a winter's day at Chelsham after withdrawal in 1980. On the far left, with much of its panelling removed, is one of the 11 AF class Northern Counties-bodied Daimler Fleetlines, diverted from Western Welsh and delivered to Godstone Garage in 1972 and usually found on the 410. In the foreground are a couple of Park Royal-bodied 45-seat AEC Reliances delivered between November 1971 and April 1972 for Green Line service: RP40 and the class pioneer, RP1. The final member of this class, RP90, has been preserved and is often seen at rallies. *M. H. C. Baker*

23

Left: RF684 outside Chelsham Garage on 4 March 1978. This was the last RF to wear the traditional Lincoln green and was withdrawn two months later. It worked the Oxted local routes and could often be seen bearing the destination Holland, which had no dykes and was a hamlet just beyond Hurst Green. *Geoff Rixon*

Below: At Gatwick Airport TD37 is seen here on the 747 Jetlink to Heathrow. Airport services assumed an ever increasing importance within the Green Line network and Jetlink would eventually be hived off as a separate company. TD37 was a Duple-bodied Leyland Tiger fitted with 46 reclining seats and is seen here shortly after delivery in 1983. *M. H. C. Baker*

Above: It had long been a tradition that at busy times — chiefly bank holidays and summer weekends — Central Area buses would help out in the Country Area. By April of 1966, when this picture of red RT1719 working the 430 in Bell Street, Reigate was taken just up the road from the garage, increasing car ownership had virtually brought this practice to an end. *Roy Hobbs*

Right: Another red bus: brand-new RML2278, this time allocated to Godstone Garage, stands at the Hardwicke Road, Reigate terminus of the 410 in October 1965. In this case its appearance is explained by the fact that not enough green RMLs were available for the complete 409/410/411 conversion and so red ones helped out for a couple of months. This batch of buses signalled the end of production of the standard RM. *Roy Hobbs*

Below: RML2336, one of the green RMLs with which Godstone Garage was long associated, passes Central Area RF387 on loan to the Country Area in Reigate, October 1967. *Roy Hobbs*

Right: RT2246 passes XA29 in Reigate, October 1967. The contrast between the refined, if by now dated, lines of the RT, and the rather less elegant provincial proportions of the Park Royal Atlantean, is striking. A batch of Atlanteans and similarly bodied Daimler Fleetlines, some in red and some in green livery, was delivered for comparison with the Routemaster. In the Country Area they operated from East Grinstead Garage, hence XA29's appearance on the 424. *Roy Hobbs*

Right: RT3725, originally delivered to Windsor Garage in June 1953, forms the centrepiece of surely the prettiest picture in the book as it climbs through the snow in Park Lane East, Reigate, close to its final home with London Country. *Roy Hobbs*

Above: Leatherhead's RT4198 and Reigate's refurbished RF78 list to starboard on the sloping forecourt of Reigate Garage in October 1967. Between August 1966 and July 1967, 174 Green Line RFs were modernised inside and out, extending their lifespan by many years. *Roy Hobbs*

Right: A defaced London Country sign, complete with 'flying Polo' emblem, outside Reigate Garage. *M. H. C. Baker*

Left: RML2330 in Lincoln green and RMC1453 in National green stand side by side on the forecourt of Reigate Garage in September 1978. Both passed to London Transport within the year and are still in existence. *Roy Hobbs*

Right: RT4344 stands outside Reigate Garage in July of 1974, probably during a crew changeover. NLP was one of the rarer LT registrations there only being two others ever to wear green livery. *Roy Hobbs*

Left: RF152 passes Woodhatch and a Ford Anglia ('any colour you like as long as its black') on its way from Luton town centre to Crawley by way of Luton, Heathrow and Gatwick Airports in the spring of 1967. *Roy Hobbs*

Right: The 425 route negotiated some very desirable Home Counties countryside on its way from Guildford to Dorking, passing quite close to the one-time home of Poet Laureate Alfred, Lord Tennyson. Seen here is RF238 *c*1970. *Geoff Lumb*

Below: A somewhat curious picture in that LNB61 posed at Nuthatch in January 1975 apparently has no owner. This is because it has just been downgraded from coach service and has the Green Line fleetname painted out. Only a Leyland or Green Line executive would have considered the sparse interiors of the Nationals with their PVC seats worthy of the definition 'coach'. *Roy Hobbs*

Right: Abinger Hammer, a much photographed spot and popular cycling territory — it once featured on the cover of the *Meccano Magazine*. RF219 passes typical North Downs tile-hung architecture on 14 April 1972. *R. C. Riley*

Left: RT3173 at rest on the forecourt of Leatherhead Garage in London Transport days, March 1967. *Roy Hobbs*

Below: Brand-new Atlantean AN126 stands outside its Leatherhead home in the early spring of 1978. The handsome Park Royal body has stood the test of time and several of this batch are still in service with London & Country as I write. *Roy Hobbs*

Left: SM459 of Addlestone about to take on board three well-bonneted ladies at Shepperton in March 1979. Addlestone Garage closed in the summer of 1997. *M. H. C. Baker*

Right: It was initially claimed that the RLH was the lowbridge version of the RT, but this was scarcely so, for it was to all intents and purposes a standard provincial Weymann-bodied AEC Mark III Regent, the first ones having originally been intended for Midland General. RLH26, seen at Guildford in April 1969, was one of the second batch, delivered in 1952. *Dave Brown*

Left: RLH24 stands at Woking in June 1969, alongside the railway station. Although the vehicles are much changed, the setting has hardly altered. *Dave Brown*

Right: RT4767 stands alongside SM101, the first of its class, at Kingston station in July 1975. RT4767, although delivered in 1954, remained in store until 1958, for London Transport had over-estimated its needs, particularly in relation to the growth of new towns, and this was one of 81 green RTs surplus to requirements. Its eventual entry into service meant the sale of an older member of the RT family. SM101 was one of the first group of new buses to enter service with London Country, in June 1970. The two-tone effect of the not very weather-resistant National leaf-green livery was one of the many less than endearing features of the Merlins and Swifts. *Geoff Lumb*

Left: RF568 basks in the autumn sun at Windsor on 6 October 1975. Delivered to Hertford in May 1953, it was withdrawn early in 1976 from Windsor Garage. *R. C. Riley*

Right: RC8 on its way from Windsor to Sevenoaks, at Olympia on 22 June 1966. The 14 RCs — AEC Reliances with Willowbrook 49-seat more or less standard provincial bodies, introduced on the 705 in November of 1965 — were the first serious attempt to replace the RF. Handsome in appearance with a striking new livery, they failed however to outlive the RF, being dogged by mechanical unreliability. They ended their passenger service days with London Country as buses in 1977. *Geoff Lumb*

Left: A wet day at Victoria, long the principal gathering point of Green Line services in central London. RF228, *en route* from Hemel Hempstead to Wrotham, takes on passengers in Buckingham Palace Road, *c*1972.
Geoff Lumb

Right: RMC1507 of Stevenage in its handsome original livery, as introduced in 1962, swings round Marble Arch on its way north in August 1965. The 68 coaches of this type were fitted with Park Royal bodies which, although of the same basic design as the red buses, had only 57 rather better padded Green Line-type seats, luggage racks, fluorescent lighting, twin headlights and a revised route destination display.
Geoff Rixon

Left: Leyland Nationals appeared on Green Line duties in 1972. Less comfortable than any of their predecessors they did nothing for the Green Line image, which was already fairly battered by competition from the private car and railway electrification. Here SNC195 departs from Eccleston Bridge on its way to Aylesbury on 16 June 1978. *R. C. Riley*

Right: 1977 saw the first real coaches, it might be argued, Green Line had ever owned. Identical to those used by National Express on its long-distance routes, they were AEC Reliances, some with Plaxton Supreme, some with Duple Dominant bodies. One of the Plaxton-bodied examples, RS107, newly delivered, stands at Eccleston Bridge bound for Aylesbury in the summer of 1979. This was one of the very last AECs ever built, for the famous Southall works closed down on 25 May 1979 and AEC production came to an end. *M. H. C. Baker*

Left: RFW3 on the forecourt of Victoria station on 28 June 1963. Fifteen of these 8ft-wide AEC Regal IVs with ECW bodywork were delivered in 1951 for the private hire fleet. These were real coaches, with 39 high-backed seats and a body design quite unlike anything else in the London Transport fleet. They were pretty unique as far as ECW was concerned too, there being just five others of this design, which went to Thomas Tilling. The RFWs never worked Green Line services, spending their entire lives on private hire duties; RFW3 was withdrawn four months after this picture was taken and all had gone by the autumn of 1964. *Geoff Lumb*

Left: Despite never achieving total success, Green Line wouldn't give up the idea of using double-deckers. Just about the most spectacular was the LRC class. These were enormous 11m-long Leyland Olympians with 72-seat ECW bodies. They were real coaches, very luxurious and designed to compete with Network SouthEast for commuter traffic. A number also went to Maidstone & District for Invictaway services from the Medway towns which, in the mid-1990s, came under the Green Line banner. By then the ECW/Olympians, like LRC4 delivered in 1983 and seen here in the Strand, would all be gone. *M. H. C. Baker*

Below: Aldgate was another long-established central London Green Line terminus, which it had shared with trolleybuses and, of course, Central Area buses. RC2, seen on the last day of the operation of this class from Grays on the 723, stands ahead of a Bow RM on 2 August 1974. *R. C. Riley*

Above: RC9, repainted into bus livery but still employed on Green Line duties, also on 2 August 1974. *R. C. Riley*

Right: RF120 was a former Green Line coach seen here at Aldgate bus station newly repainted in light National green and bright yellow and still employed on Green Line duties in 1974, after 22 years service. It was withdrawn in April 1977. *R. C. Riley*

Below: 1980 marked the Golden Jubilee of Green Line and much was made of it. A number of the latest coaches appeared in a special golden livery. Duple-bodied Reliance RB135 is seen here on an excursion to Bournemouth on the site of the town's old West station in the summer of that year. *M. H. C. Baker*

Right: RT3315 looks out of its Grays home into the winter sun two days before Christmas 1974. Routemasters had, by this date, officially taken over all scheduled double-deck workings and RT3315 was filling in; a chronic shortage of spare parts meant that many Routemasters were off the road. *R. C. Riley*

Left: A fairly unexpected purchase in 1974, for use as trainers, were four AEC Reliances with Harrington Wayfarer Cavalier coach bodies. These had gone into service with Maidstone & District in 1962. T3, seen here at Grays on 23 December 1974, entered preservation in 1978, but had gone for scrap by 1987. *R. C. Riley*

Below left: As part of the National Bus Company it was perhaps inevitable that London Country would eventually finish up with ECW-bodied Bristol VRs in its fleet. It bought 15 in 1977 and sent them to Grays, although I did see one on the A25 near Godstone before it entered passenger service. BT6 is seen here at Grays alongside a couple of Nationals in February 1980. The class was quite quickly sold to the Bristol Omnibus Company, but London & Country later owned some similar second-hand examples. *D. T. Elliott*

Right: A class much beloved by enthusiasts is the GS. Eighty-four of these little Guys with 26-seat ECW bodies entered service from 1953, replacing prewar Leyland Cubs. Style-wise they were a curious but successful mixture of Fordson lorry front end, standard ECW side view and LT rear. Like a number of the class, the pioneer, GS1, has been beautifully preserved. The 393 was one of many low-density routes which the class worked. Eventually they were either replaced by bigger buses or the routes were abandoned. *M. H. C. Baker*

Left: SNB228 poses prettily outside Epping station on 29 October 1980. Views on whether Nationals really do look pretty vary greatly, but they have certainly proved long-lived. London Country owned more of them in their various forms than any other company and a good many are still serving its successors. Epping station had been built in the 19th century by the Great Eastern Railway; it was taken over by London Transport upon the extension of the Central Line to Epping in 1949. The steam shuttle service to Ongar was replaced by electric trains in 1957, but this service was abandoned in 1994, but is the subject of a preservation attempt. *R. C. Riley*

Below: Stevenage Garage in May 1971. Letchworth, which is RF691's next destination, was the northernmost extremity reached by London's green buses, some 35 miles north of 55 Broadway. The vivid yellow applied by London Country when it took over from London Transport certainly brightened things up, although it wasn't to everyone's taste. *Geoff Lumb*

Above: Some very interesting things happened at Stevenage as the 1960s gave way to the 1970s. A survey carried out in the new town calculated that it would be cheaper to run a subsidised bus service compared to undertaking extensive new road building and thus on 29 December 1969, in one of its last acts before London Country took over, London Transport introduced the Blue Arrow service. There were two routes, publicised as 'personal taxis' for commuters, operated by three repainted Daimler Fleetlines. XF8 is seen ahead of an RT on 6 September 1971. *R. C. Riley*

Right: Revisions took place and in 1971 five Swifts and two Metro-Scania single-deckers, painted in a vivid yellow and royal blue livery, inaugurated the Superbus network. However, there was still work for traditional London Country vehicles as can be seen in this September 1971 view of SM498 and RT4038 at Stevenage bus station. *R. C. Riley*

Left: RTs and SMs worked alongside each other on the 809. SM485 looks positively immaculate in May 1971. *R. C. Riley*

Below: The very first London Country Leyland Nationals were sent to Stevenage. LN7 in green livery on the left and LN3 in Superbus livery, both of which entered service in December 1972, are seen at the bus station in November 1977. Creeping into the picture on the left is an Atlantean in green livery, but bearing the SB logo. *M. H. C. Baker*

Below: RMC4 at its Hatfield home in November 1977. This is the famous prototype Routemaster coach, introduced into Green Line service in October 1957. Prototypes in any transport field do not tend to have very long lives in normal service, and its three fellows, RMs 1, 2 and 3, although all still in existence, did very little regular passenger work. RMC4 was the exception for, after eight years on Green Line service, it worked as a bus from Hatfield longer than any other Routemaster, not being withdrawn until 1 May 1979. *M. H. C. Baker*

Right: Unlike nearly all its brothers RMC4 was not sold back to London Transport, but was proudly kept as a display bus. Here it is, back in Green Line livery but with later modifications, looking quite splendid at Cobham in March 1995. *M. H. C. Baker*

Above: Metro-Cammell-bodied Scania MS1 is looking less than pristine at Stevenage in November 1977. Although popular with passengers, there were maintenance problems with the Swedish buses and they were sold shortly afterwards. However, they were the first of the many buses of Scandinavian origin which are now so familiar on the routes once served by London's green buses. *M. H. C. Baker*

Left: SMW6 passing St Albans Abbey on 10 June 1975. This was one of 15 AEC Swifts which originally entered service with South Wales Transport but were transferred to London Country in 1971. It had Marshall 53-seat bodywork. The SMWs, like all the Swifts, were not greatly loved, and served less than 10 years, SMW6 going to C. F. Booth for scrap in December 1981. *R. C. Riley*

Right: We have looked at the three Chelsham RTs repainted in full National livery, but Hertford also had one so adorned, although it was never used in passenger service. Here it is, RT2367, seen outside St Albans Garage on 10 June 1975. It had acquired National livery in January of that year. As I write, attempts are being made to preserve St Albans as a typical London Country garage. *R. C. Riley*

343 via St. Albans
DUNSTABLE SQUARE
343 via Flamstead
ST ALBANS CITY

LONDON COUNTRY

GREEN LINE

PAY AS YOU ENTER
PLEASE

MLL 593

Far left: Refurbished coach RF206 is still carrying Green Line livery along with London Country's 'flying Polo' symbol, although demoted to bus work. It is parked outside St Albans Garage awaiting its next journey to Dunstable in May 1973. It was withdrawn 11 months later. *Geoff Lumb*

Left: One of the most famous green bus routes north of the river was the 301 which ran northwest from Watford up the A41 alongside the Grand Union Canal and the West Coast main line, veering slightly further to the west at Tring, and on to Aylesbury. Its blinds are carried by ST821, the only standard example of its class to be preserved, seen on one of its rare outings from its home in the London Transport Museum at Covent Garden, at Brighton in May 1990. STs, which were short-length AEC Regents, went into service with the National Company, a London General subsidiary, in 1930. ST821 was first registered on 2 March 1931 at Watford, the National headquarters, and spent all its life in the Country Area until replaced by RTs in May 1949. It is almost identical to its red brothers except for the route indicator and, of course, livery. *M. H. C. Baker*

Below: RT3816 at the Aylesbury terminus of the 301 in July 1969. A Thames Valley Bristol FLF Lodekka stands behind. *Geoff Lumb*

Left: The autumn sun shines on RT1015, with London Country lettering and yellow stripe, as it waits for a new crew outside Tring Garage in October 1972 before continuing its journey northwards. *Dave Brown*

Right: The 301 remained RT-operated longer than many London Country routes but by 1975 Leyland Nationals had taken over. SNB93, originally a coach delivered in 1973, but soon downgraded to bus work, is seen at Hemel Hempstead in the summer of 1975. *M. H. C. Baker*

Below: Whilst not every enthusiast's favourite bus, the Leyland National has proved to be long-lived, certainly being a good deal more reliable than its London Country Swift predecessors. SNB357, delivered to London Country in 1976, is seen (this time south of the Thames in Oxted) in the attractive London & Country livery 20 years later. *M. H. C. Baker*

Left: Garston Garage at Watford in March 1979. Nearest the camera is MBS298, still in Lincoln green livery but with National-style fleetname. Behind are RMLs, the furthest from the camera looking far from healthy.
It was the sale of 17 London Country Routemasters to Wombwell Diesels for scrap in March 1979 which prompted London Transport to step in and buy as many RMLs, RMCs and RCLs as it could get its hands on. *M. H. C. Baker*

Right: AN42 at St Albans on 10 June 1975. This was one of the first batch of Atlanteans which entered service with London Country in 1972. They had Park Royal 72-seat bodywork and introduced one-person double-deck operation on a large scale, following the pioneering efforts of the XFs and XAs. *R. C. Riley*

Above: BL22, delivered in October 1973, and RF575, delivered in June 1953, stand outside Amersham Garage in May 1974. *Geoff Lumb*

Right: The 309 wended its way through outer-suburban Middlesex and Buckinghamshire along the edge of the Central Area; when new in 1935, a Q on this route would have met up at Uxbridge with former London United tram Route 7 which also terminated there and which, in its final years, was worked by the impressive Felthams. The Qs were remarkable buses: side-engined AECs a

decade ahead of their time. London Transport bought 238 of them in various guises and they lasted until 1952/3. Q55 was one of 102 4Q4s fitted with BRWC 35-seat bodies. Although mostly Country Area buses, 27 were used for a time in the late 1930s as Green Line coaches. Q55 is seen at the Science Museum outstation at Wroughton, near Swindon. It is standing alongside TF77, an equally unusual vehicle: a 34-seat LPTB-bodied Green Line coach mounted on a Leyland Tiger underfloor-engine chassis dating from 1939. *M. H. C. Baker*